TOURIST TO THE SUN

A poetry collection

Virginia Betts

Tim Saunders Publications

CONTENTS

Title Page

Introduction

Foreword

TOURIST TO THE SUN   1

Tourist to the sun   2

Drifter   4

Space Junk   6

Lost Property   8

Drowning Day   10

Dysmorphic   12

Cryonic   14

Visibility, poor   16

One Moment   18

Families, caught   20

My Love Is Pure   24

Talking about art   26

Comeback   29

Masking	32
Spaces	35
Shadows	37
Echo	39
An Afternoon Walk	41
When Birds Sing Sweetly	44
Night Shadow	46
Memory Box	47
Bridges	49
The Uninvited Guest	51
Summer's Gone	52
Two benches	54
Missing Persons	55
Birthday	56
On the disused airfield	57
Sleeping	59
Time's Terrain	61
Home Revisited	63
Ghosts	65
Stepping Out On Derby Day	67
Natasha	69
Eleventh Hour	71
Apple Splinter	73
The Hunted Down	75

Forest 77

Invasion 78

Westminster Bridge 2020 80

Flesh and Glass 82

Two Haiku 84

Tanka 85

Church doors 86

Swimming 89

Waited, I did 90

Waiting Water 92

In My Shoes 94

Tim Saunders Publications 97

INTRODUCTION

Virginia Betts is a tutor, writer and actor from Ipswich, Suffolk. Her stories and poems have been published in books, literary magazines and aired on BBC Radio. She collaborated with Hightide Theatre Company and The Wolsey Theatre on a short play about lockdown, *Lullaby*, and her first book of short stories, *The Camera Obscure,* will be published in 2022. Virginia played the lead in The Suffolk Poetry Society's *All Change*, a play in verse by Peter Sandberg in their annual festival in 2022, and is currently rehearsing for *The Neurodiversity Launch Pad*. She is working on her second collection of stories, a novel. Virginia has a particular interest and skill in helping neurodiverse learners in her tuition work, because she is autistic, which was diagnosed when she was an adult. Virginia is married with one son, aged 21.

FOREWORD

Poetry flows from the soul. It is an intensely emotional form of communication and as with all art forms, it is subjective. I enjoy reading poetry, from Betjeman, Housman and Guest, to more contemporary writers. I write it myself.

In my experience it is rare for a poet to write a collection that grips the reader from beginning to end; it's a very difficult thing to achieve. However, I feel that Virginia Betts has managed to do just that.

By having a strong underlying theme on which to hang her variety of work, she has held my attention with a mix of traditional poetry, haiku and even an excellent sea shanty.

I consider myself extremely fortunate to have discovered Virginia.

Tim Saunders
Editor

TOURIST TO THE SUN

A poetry collection

To Helen,

Enjoy this!
I'd love to read yours.

Virginia Betts

TOURIST TO THE SUN

Fired-up for take-off,
wearing my asbestos suit, designed to deflect,
I bring with me a cabin full of unmarked
baggage for the hold.

Wing walker without a rope,
hurtling to the light fantastic,
untethered.

First to sign up to step off the map;
where even the silvery surface is
marked by dark spots;
even the brightest star is already dead.

With outstretched arms I
surrender to the sun,
glide, star-shaped, licked by flicking
tongues of flame,
into the white-hot core;
white heat devouring sound,
eclipsing time,
searing conscience and

annihilating thought.

Not arrogance that brings me here,
but fear.
The elemental need to fly, unfettered,
to pilot my own craft;
to pierce reality,
and seek the truth behind it,
and, in seeking, half expect to find it.

And thus, avoiding bird-strikes,
negotiate safe water-landings
when at last I am earthbound;
within my hand,
a brand to fire my piece of earth's story

when I return
scorched and burned.

DRIFTER

I could float away -
Drift across the universe,
Wonder if it's all been worth
Anything.

I could travel up through time and space,
Unravel, like a ball of wool,
Disintegrate and crumble
Into dust.

I would tumble like an astronaut,
Tethered to a shining cord,
Collapsing in upon myself,
Swallowing the endless breath of time.

I could smile so hard-
Colour in between the lines,
Pick glass fragments from my mind,
Stumble on a ragged block
Of truth.

I might stow away,
Shooting up beyond the stars,
Shredding paper-darted years,
Stealing buried treasure,

Like loot.

I should hammer home,
Falling through the atmosphere,
Shielded by a web of fear,
Peeling back skin layers
Like fruit.

SPACE JUNK

I don't know what the astronaut dreams,
does he cut the cord
and float downstream?

Does he drift away on a honeyback cloud?
Does he ride the wave
of electric sound?

Will he pierce the bubble of a sharp-edged lie
With a sonar radar
In a herringbone sky?

Can he climb the ladder to a shooting star,
and spiral-snake back
for a day trip to Mars?

Will he risk colliding with the junk in space,
blinded by refracted light
distorting his face?

The only sounds he hears have already gone
rebounding back
in an echoing song.

Will he fall to earth on a stardust trail
When the pale blue dot

Begins to dilate?

Will you always travel to the end of the path
where the grass grows long,
and lights have gone out?

And as time bends double with a heavy head,
petrol-coloured diamonds
are words unsaid.

LOST PROPERTY

If I collected all the lost keys –
the ones on rings, or chains,
that drop into drains,
unclaimed,
and squat there,
sequestered out of sight,
rusting behind bars,
far below blue sky,
in dank, stale beds,
just beyond light;

all the buttons, hanging by a thread,
that fall, unnoticed,
and fag-ends, and bits of cotton gone astray;
credit cards,
slipped slyly from shallow pockets;
lipstick, abandoned by a sink-side;
drawing pins and tacks that nestle in soft pile
poised to pounce,
and pierce the flesh of hand or foot

like nails,
evading hammers,
spiralling from empty shelves

dropped down loudly
to swearing curses;
under sofas, between cracks,
rogue staples worked free,
sending loose leaves
scattered to the wind;

If I could gather these,
place winking silver coins
beside the rest;
create small change;
collect them in a shiny tin;

then I might thread the needle,
mend the holes,
pay my debts,
unlock all the doors,
and let the world back in.

DROWNING DAY

It isn't the incessant ticking of two clocks,
out of sync;
or the intermittent roar of angry boiler
firing up;
nor constant, never-ending whine
that bleats my name, demands my time,
and bursts my thoughts
with shards of irritation
like fibreglass on skin,
dissolving them to nothing more
than distant echoes drifting
on the wind.

Nor is it the constant trill and beep-
vibrating buzz on desktop;
wrong numbers hurriedly picked up,
hung up, left hanging on an empty line.

And not the day itself,
though in its grey parade,
soundless clouds steal thunder,
stifling spring with shadows.

But something stops me in my tracks;

holds me up at gunpoint;
hijacks me; arrests me;
comes crashing through
to storm my senses -

Invisible giant!
Sends me running from the house;
fall writhing on the ground,
head in hands,
scream without a sound,
as if floored by some corrosive douse -

to suffer
the searing sound of wrong notes played
Again
Again...

Out of tune

Going down

Surrounded

I drown.

DYSMORPHIC

Nobody hates me more than
my own worst enemy.
Can't even cry;
don't want to say.

My face in the back of a spoon,
upside-down, reflected back, distorted,
like a clownish cartoon.
Huge-eyed fly can't settle.

Magnified five times,
I disappear.
Examine fine lines
that turn into crevices
hiding secrets.

Like thin, grey elastic,
I am over-washed;
over-stretched.
Tiny fibres spring loose and fray,
Pinging coils like serpent tongues.

The mirror sends back distress signals,
warping flesh into dough,
spilling out,

when only yesterday,
bones jutted like
splayed rudders.

No anchor. Sharp thought assaulted,
whip-lashed by bright white spikes.
Bed of nails, grown numb,
So over-used.

Perhaps hide, wrapped within
my thick, black habit,
While this disease
brings me to my knees.

Silence the swarming
crackle of brain on fire,
dragging disorder into chaos.

One last black look
before I head off.

CRYONIC

You keep me in suspended animation;
like an unborn;
splay me out long-limbed;
your experiment;
home is your laboratory.

Tied to you by invisible thread;
you reel me in with a flick,
and throw me back, cold.

You galvanise me;
poke me with sticks;
see if I twitch.

Bombard me with flowers
shower me with stars;
bury me under lilies;
under willow, hide my light,
cable-tied.
Flood me with energy;
Resist me.

You bruise me.
Take me to your mirror;
Show me a reflection of you;

Drink me in and drag me through,

Until I disappear;
Only an assembly of parts.
My creator,
you hold my heart.

You make me your creature,
Leave me to die in a frozen wilderness;
Devour me whole;
Falling;
Onward we go;
Archangel -
You rip out my soul.

VISIBILITY, POOR

The general synopsis at 0600:

Shannon, Forties;
veering south from time to time -
depression.
5 to 7 -
rough, occasionally VERY rough.
Becoming high later;
occasionally poor.

Trafalgar, 9
easterly, veering north easterly,
backing south;
squally showers soon.
Moderate.

Fastnet;
decreasing soon;
backing 3 or 4;
rain imminent.
Poor.

Dogger;
rapidly moving;
becoming cyclonic at first;
decreasing later.

Slightly high;
showers soon.
Mainly fair.

Irish Sea Viking;
Thames Fisher
backing west;
occasional severe gale,
becoming rough soon.
Thundery. Occasionally,
fog.

Fair Isle,
sole
very rapidly veering south,
becoming slight.
Extensive fog; snow imminent.
Poor.

Losing its identity.

ONE MOMENT

All day, the low hum of suburban sounds;
The children's laughter catches on the breeze,
Punctuated by sharp, staccato shrieks.
A distant dog barks and an engine whines.

Somewhere, behind closed doors
and shuttered blinds,
Mother in perpetual withdrawal,
Hiding behind the fringes of her life.
Somewhere, a young boy crosses the street.

And if ever the universe conspired
With time, this was the moment where they met,
Whispered plans, fingers poised to join.
Two points lightly touch; electric charge spits.

A shattering collision, this moment
Entwining of co-incidence and chance,
But was catalysed antecedently,
When intervention took him from his home.

Took no time to reach a snap decision,
Resting on the landing of the coin's spin,
To keep him safe, they took him somewhere else:
To Dad, who smashed Mum in the mouth.

Not Dad's fault, he had a dreadful childhood.
And he could give his boy better, no doubt.
He didn't want him to have what he had,
Where he was dragged up but somehow survived.

Behind his own blinds, shuttered, he's sprawled out,
His secret sleeps in a can and a syringe.
But money talks and his mouth was loudest,
His pale paunch concealed beneath a stale suit.

And now, as crowds gather round, the boy bleeds.
Ambulance chasers stand and
gawp, loose-mouthed.
Who can say if this is how it should end?
Or if another time or place would mend?

FAMILIES, CAUGHT

Today, in court 3,
a judge stole my son.

He knew nothing about me,
or our lives and how far we'd come.
All he had were some pieces of paper,
written by a couple of women,
both named Claire.

About how I'd been beaten
and tried not to show it;
diminished with words;
and although I knew it,
I hadn't the voice
to articulate pain;
easier to keep the peace,
to people-please, like a good woman should,
to let him bring me to my knees,
weighed down by gaudy gifts
and promises he'd never keep.

Somewhere in those years,

where I wasn't free,
just a poor, peroxide, imitation of me;
high flying trophy-wife;
I watched myself glide by
as I stood,
a passive observer
of my own life.

And in those pages
All that was missing.
Distilled down
To a few brutal, sordid sentences
Of victim-blaming shame.

That I *failed to protect*
from a thing I could not see,
as if it was so easy -
it was bigger than me.
That I *ignored the severity*
and played down the rows;
encouraged my children
to *accept his abuse*;
they said
I had *no insight;*
I *failed*, they said.

And although he took my life,
my job, my home and self-belief,
it didn't stop there;

because I had left,
I had to be punished
and hung out to dry;

and so, he enlisted the powers-that-be
to enable more beatings
Without touching me.

They blindly accepted his crocodile smile;
he bought them with Gucci and honey
the watches and suits,
and the sweet scent of money.

He *is* an abuser, (they stated that clearly);
but *you* are the cause by failing to see
how bad he could be.
And complaints and letters
and all your whining
about the injustice,
well, it makes it so obvious -
you are a hysterical, chaotic mess.
And so our conclusion:
it's all for the best
that he takes his son
away from you, too
with full power
to do what he likes to you.

So they said he'd be fair;
that he'd changed his ways;
that I needed to see that,
and be his best friend,
for the sake of the child
I would not see again.

But it is not just my voice
crying out in the dark;

hundreds of mothers, and fathers too;
broken hearts bleeding and crushed
in the dust;
trying to do our best
in this witch-hunting,
broken system;
failing our children,
and failing us.

MY LOVE IS PURE

She has sapphire magpie wings
falling in sheets of silk;
pale as death and fragile
as a cloud dissolved in mist.

She is amber wind,
spins hypnotic whirling dance,
black as a raven in her soul
and silver-lined like heaven's walls.

She has a splintered egg-shell heart;
makes music like the gods.
She stirs the leaves; she lifts the waves;
Deep as a well; un-touched.

Always scratching at your core;
never enough; wanting more.
When she's gone you cry her back
When she's back, you hate her.

She will hush a lullaby,
drift you down in feather bed.
But hollow dreams are all she brings;
she's always in your head.

Broken feather; angel wings
driven, like the slush in snow.
Nothing ever makes her go,
although she's gone by morning.

I love her with my hollow bones;
I love her with my ragged face;
I'd give her everything I own
If she would stay this moment.

Tragic face on silver screen;
dying swan; tormented scene;
and just as swift, a peaceful dream;
she wraps you up in linen sheets.

Always scratching at your core;
Never enough; wanting more.
That's how you know your love is pure;
And that is why you hate her.

TALKING
ABOUT ART

Amsterdam, 1995

When they look at us,
they will see two beers,
a boy and a girl in a café,
talking about art.

Nothing unusual in that, in this city;
city of art and museums,
café culture, smoking coffee-shops, late night buses,
trams deliver to your destination;
noise and tourist crowds at Centraal Station,
where tie-dyed back-packers arrive stoned
and seek retreat in *Rasta-baby*; Bulldogs
who think they've found the answers

in this city of vice;
where she learned a lesson
about love, and life,
many years before she was a wife.

I can still hear the clock-bell chime now.
I can still see what they see -

they don't notice the dark domestic
drama playing out
in this tiny, wax-scented bar,
memories of minus 9 in winter,
but cold still this summer, in The Heights;
Closes at 2am; closed now forever.

Been back this year -
from a better place; grown-up son in tow;
showed him where I used to go.

But still, some secrets stay forever trapped
at that shiny, beer-soaked table,
in that mirrored bar;
a tiny piece of time, blinking on and off
like the red neon lights.

They don't notice she's already crying,
that something far too big to tell
is already dying;
that between them, all they have grown
is a ghost.

We skirt around the issue;
anything but that.
And even now she knows that she
will feel the sting in years to come;

A scar will sear for twenty years,
And steer all her wrong turns
and walks down unlit paths.

Yet still we invest in our pretence to be
exactly what they seem to see -

Just a boy and a girl in a café,
talking about art,
waiting to part.

COMEBACK

You announced it
three weeks before you came back.

We tingled with anticipation;
almost tasting the sensation of the past;
re-creating fragments of truthful mythology
left to fester over fifteen years.

We carry on where we left off;
strange bending of time,
where we are twenty-four again-
faking faces
and parking by the sea,
filling spaces
in abandoned places.

Peeling-paint café; chips and smoke;
dancing to the tune of our own
silent disco:
Happy Mondays, Eight-Day Weeks,
and boring Sundays.

Discomfort, though, in this turn-about of time.
Unspoken; awkward;
have we left too much behind?

We reclaim shadows of our former selves,
recreating old photographs
with curled edges,
faded by eternal sunlight,
and yellow-stained;
chemical smiles melt like wax
under scrutiny's heated gaze.

You ease disjointedly back
Into a shape, which has altered.
The picture you vacated
re-formed;
untraceable;

leaves us standing on the perimeter,
in no man's land,
eases us to the side of our friendly match.

And now you've gone, I wonder

if I should have made more effort…
and why there is relief
at the leaving,
instead of grief.

Odd anti-climax,
like a long-awaited show.
Should I have stalled,
on hold?
I don't know.

As you slide back

to your other life,
where the strange is familiar
and my absence commonplace,
I'm almost certain of a fact:

that little is lost in leaving;
more in the coming back.

MASKING

We meet in the street;
you fancy a chat,
and you go on and on
about this,
and that;
I admire your coat;
you admire mine;
I say you seem tired;
you say you'd look better
if you'd had the time,
this morning,
to put your face on.

To put your face on
means make-up;
like after a fight;
so maybe a *brave face*;
which is *war-paint*;
which then leads to *Braveheart*,
smeared and daubed,
leading the charge;
so, leads charging;
well, there's my laptop

at home, charging up,
like a knight on a white horse-
or *loitering alone* -
like the one in Keats' poem,
where things *wither by the lake*;
which leads to monsters of the deep,
though technically that's a *loch*,
like in a door,
without a key;
stop, stop, stop!

A quay!
Where War-Brides stand
to wave goodbye to their sweet heartland -
and your remark makes my thoughts take off;
spill into my brain
in split-second time,
and, as they take flight,
I miss your next lines.

So, I just keep quiet,
and nod and smile
in the right place, I hope;
put on a made-up face;
wear normality like a cloak;

play out the elaborate spectacle
of the mask,
while behind the crafted veneer,
bottomless wells of thoughts
spiral down endlessly,
and the grey shadow of fatigue

follows fast.

SPACES

Some spaces
pocket air for energy;
gain strength from solid emptiness
surrounded by more spaces;
withstand any blow.

And spaces left
when bricks and concrete crumble;
drift down on a breath
melt away, like snow.

Blank spaces hang in air
when crystal stars explode
and radiate brief pinpoint glory -
then fall and disappear.

There are spaces too, on sofas;
between us; within us;
spaces left in rooms vacated
by recently departed
from empty beds
still warm from lying in.

Spaces between steps mark time
and trace the empty hours

between tidal waves of guilt.

Spaces that we visit
in darkening hours of day
when twilight falls in muted grey,
and night's shadow follows fast -

these spaces form tears
that even sleep's seamstress cannot mend;
nor time unbend.

SHADOWS

A sunny sky will always yield shadows,
which creep insidiously,
arms outstretched,
spread long
to suck the colour from the scene.

Shadows soon bring thunder
to split the dome in darkening hours
and cloud grey skies in June;
releasing rain
in sharp spears
which shred the fragile bloom.

And shapes, seemingly so solid,
dissolve
like liquid gold
and melt away,

receding backwards into night
to shoot up skywards
like mercury in flight
and then constrict,
shrinking down
to a single

blue dot
on an infinite black canvas;
smothered by shadows
and riddled with holes.

ECHO

A web waves in the warm breeze,
caught between ancient wooden struts,
indefensible, beneath an empty seat.
It splays to breaking point;
fine-knit, like a fibre-glass veil;
delicate strength resisting air.

Behind, purple bell-shaped blooms
bow their heads in unison,
deferring to the weight
of a sprinkler's misty jet,
that fans out in the shape of victory.

But it is not these shimmering droplets
that crystallise quietness;
nor the opaque haze,
as heat warps the scene into film;
it is not even the web, hanging on, precarious,
like angel-hair, suspended,
where even one breath might fracture the whole.

My quiet distils
to single drips
echoing inside a hollow barrel,

like an insistent broken tap
in a sleeping house at midnight,
incessantly filling night's spaces
until dawn arrives again.

AN AFTERNOON WALK

It is after midday,
And, filled with wine and warm food,
We flatten the wet grass
With clumsy trudge.

Leaves reveal the sun's prismatic flashes,
Intermittent arrows that offer
Blind comfort.

The damp air smells of twilight,
Though the day's hardly done.
And each stone, weather-worn,
Deflects a close inspection,
In shades of shadowy blue.

We tiptoe around the grassy mounds,
I, imagining the shivering rows, turning,
Where we step,
Disturbed.

We hold hands, but I am
Not there.

I think I hear ancient hymns drift and catch
On the breeze,
And whispered voices slip from slumber,
Diffuse across time, without words.

All that remains is a feeling.
The chipped and crumbling stone fragments;
My thoughts dissemble into shards
On the grass.

And I am in this earth -
This soft, brown, enveloping ground,
Absorbed,
Where no light or sound
Can reach me.

This strange, bleak and hollow silence,
Surrounds me fold on fold,
Where no bird sings,
And stories never told
Fight to surface.

I hear the distant mower drone,
And lamb bleats murmur,
While high above, an engine of the past
Hums peacefully across the sky,
The thin smoke trail connecting you, and I

To be wrapped within this silent world;
To cease to be;
Where all deeds die,
And somehow slip away

In time, we are all just stories;

Our vain attempts to make our mark,
Melt like sandstone in rain;
Like chalk into dust.

Our names carved in art
Fail to be indelible,
And who knows
Who lies here?

Our fingers find their meeting point.
I think this moment should be suspended.
For jealous time trivialises the relentless
Crawl upon the wheel,
And shatters us,
Scattering our thoughts to be blown to the wind.

WHEN BIRDS SING SWEETLY

When birds sing sweetly,
bright notes fall on deaf ears.

My sightless sockets
no longer watch the setting sun descend
in orange splendour
behind purple hills.
My fleshless limbs reach, suspended
in un-returned embrace,
and hope sleeps in earth's damp bed.

I once walked in your place, above,
treading soft amongst the stones,
my mind fixed firmly on the stars;
warm wind stroked my face,
framed by a pale blue sky.

I gave no thought to those below;
long chains of lives laid out in rows.
I brushed aside insistent whispers,
growing louder year on year;
Time's breath at my back,

closing in an ever-shortening shadow.

I am so close I could call out to you -
stretch up to grasp your ankles as you pass;
but my soundless cries are impotent
as dust on stone
scattered by the merest breath of air;
all thoughts dissolved
in earth,
and flesh to grass.

NIGHT SHADOW

Tonight I will dream of the fox;
the shape of a dart;
shadowy figure shoots
through shaded glades;
stalks between trees;
slips across the ancient
ribbon of a stream;
midnight scavenger
steals like a thief,
unseen.

Monochrome phantom of the night,
Never viewed in colour,
As nature's bloom bursts bright.

But tonight I will dream of the fox;
dainty steps weave through waving reeds;
fragile thin-faced knave makes dusty tracks.
When day unwinds,
he will dance across the landscape
of my mind.

MEMORY BOX

Every now and then,
I open the box,
pick the lock,
prize up the lid,
and take stock.

My face is bathed in a golden light,
as, pirate-like, I survey this treasure
of things that mean something.

A ticket-stub kept for twenty years,
from the last time you were here.
Touch its dry and yellowing card,
hear the hum of pulsating beat,
your sweet-bitter voice, when you leave.

Festival flyer
from another decade,
brings back the strength and heat
of the sun which burned all year,
it seemed,
as we swayed to the rhythm,
and dreamed.

Picture postcards of

framed thoughts
with frayed edges;
windy sea-shell smiles;
sand-brushed day trips;
nights explored.

Your voice drowned by wind;
your face paled by snow;
your letters scattered leaves;
this box;
these ashes.

BRIDGES

There are some bridges
you never cross when you come to them.

Perhaps you turn around;
leave it for another day
which never arrives;
it's never the time.

But if now is not the time,
when is?

When all your ducks are standing neatly
in a line?
When heavens, stars and planets
are cosmically aligned?
When all the angry ghosts surround you,
upbraiding you
for allowing days to slip by in a haze,
while the clock ticks ever faster
from its glass-walled cage?

Because you need to know
the terrifying truth,
and fury
of reaching your last page,

hoping you have time to start again,
and finding all your bridges burned
before you reach them.

THE UNINVITED GUEST

Age arrives unexpectedly,
like the unwelcome guest at a party
loitering on your doorstep in the rain.

Flouncing in
like she owns the place; vandalising your space.
Eviction is impossible; despite a valiant fight,
she squats stubbornly
holding you to ransom;
inhabiting corners like a churlish surprise.
Spiteful old maid.

Ghostly shadow of you;
ransacking youth;
Time's most accomplished
accomplice
steals your reflection;
subdues you finally into silence.

SUMMER'S GONE

a song

Turning on the sunshine in my brain,
Wishing things could always stay the same,
Killing time when time is running out,
Slipping off the window-ledge of doubt.

Weeding out the cotton edge of truth,
Raking up the frayed threads hanging loose,
Smiling from the corners of my mind,
Peeping out, afraid what I might find.

You pace time,
I sometimes wish that something
would astound me.
Read my mind,
And slide on my own ashes that surround me.

Making judgements, playing fast and loose,
Bailing out, confronting my own truth,
Losing time, distorting all the facts,
Twisting my reflection, mirror's black.

We waste time,
We slip and slide on skirted interactions.
Climb inside,

The prism of a crystalised refraction.

Oh, the summer's running out,
Oh, the summer's running out,
Oh, the summer's dying out.

Summer's gone,
Summer's gone.

TWO BENCHES

I never imagined this.
Outside a blank, white room,
with its blank, white walls.
Inside, the clock unwinds;
seconds drip steadily down the line,
waiting for nature to call time.

On a cold metallic bench
I wait, suspended;
Stop-motion faces speed by;
nothing changes,
but nothing is the same.

Streaming in, glassy light is prismed
through the pane;
the sky bright and empty;
seagulls scream silently;
white ornamental frieze, framed against the blue.

And later, on a broken bench in the bay,
I watch the white-topped waves
constantly returning home;
still in the blank, white room;
still seeing your blank, wide stare.

MISSING
PERSONS

You joined the missing persons list this year.
It seems you've left a hole too big to
fill; too deep to climb in.
And where do all the missing persons go
when you can't find them?

The seasons are so full of empty spaces
and my mind is crowded noisily with
half-remembered faces
as I return in quietness to long forgotten places.

Time's tide is unrelenting in its haste
to wash away the pages of brief chapters.
No photograph can outrun time's indecent pace;
our minds can only colour in the
scenes of ever-afters.

And, after all, time spent has fragile recompense;
breakable as thin, translucent, eggshell skin;
paper-fine and dry as ancient parchment
on which records a lifetime of events.

BIRTHDAY

Above the seared, red grass,
That dances to the rhythm of the wind,
Storm clouds circle
Like the beginning of life.
Fibres dropped in fluid,
Splayed webbed mesh,
Allowing disconnected glances
Of splintered light.

Two tiny birds,
Reflected in the rear-view mirror,
Take flight;
Vying for supremacy in the scattered blue,
Above a yellow Piper Cub,
A pink rose in its cockpit
To remember you.

ON THE DISUSED AIRFIELD

Watching the shadows of the clouds
move across the grass,
I am reminded of the movement of the sea.
The way that timelessness is held
within a rolling wave
as it drifts in perpetual motion
towards eternity.
That time's soft and ceaseless steps
slide by unnoticed,
and its rhythms are expressed within each
single blade of grass,
casts a strange shadow over me, too.

The low drone of the distant engines,
partnered by the muffled roar of wind,
suspend the moment in time's teardrop;
the colours run in the heat-hazed horizon
and the ghost of old engine-fuelled adrenaline
takes flight once more.
The echo of a memory sits somewhere
on the edge of today's crisp outline

and the fragile minute fleetingly touches fingertips
to hold hands with the past.

SLEEPING

Near sleeping now,
I think of you.
Grey shapes drift in and out,
formless, nameless,
almost-faces;
indistinct memories
of half-forgotten places.

I want to curl my hand once more
around your finger,
like I did in times before;
when anything would make you smile
and you so fragile, my only fear
that you would break,
and even sleeping time was time
that time could never
separate.

Small hands build strong lives;
and touching yours once more,
my tears form.
I want to find the strength to let you go,
I hope I let you know I am still here;

trying to reach across the space between us.

Always.

TIME'S TERRAIN

Nervously, I make my way across the room,
Braving the terrain of No Man's Land.
I take your hand,
You stand.

Gingerly, I slide my hand across the bed,
Navigating oceans of thick fleece.
I touch your feet.
You sleep.

Achingly, I look across to feel your smile,
Wishing I could halt the hands of time.
You falter.
Things alter.

Haltingly, I make my way across the floor,
Shuffling through the changing pace of time,
You in your bed,
I in mine.

Cautiously, I reach across to take your hand,
Pondering the long, unbroken lines.
This is your time,
Not mine.

Shakily, I wheel myself across the tiles,
Crossing the abyss from bed to door.
There's no bed for you
Anymore.

Finally, I take a journey one last time,
Carried to the strange, uncharter'd land.
You take my hand.
We stand.

HOME REVISITED

The trees that were planted
no longer bear fruit.
The garden looks haunted
by plans left undone.

Old tools lying scattered
No seeds in the ground;
Gaunt house sits abandoned,
as if sick with plague.

Years since I was here;
Grey walls, bare of frames;
Dark, empty spaces
Are all that remain.

A house wrapped in ivy,
Which strangles all dreams,
is tangled in memories
which might have been.

I touch the dry walls;
Run fingers through dust;
Piano keys tinkle,
But the tune is lost.

Flies gather aimlessly
around rotting remains;
hollow laughter echoes
through star-shattered panes.

Snow falling heavily
settles so fast.
I sleep suspended
in dreamless, blank space.

GHOSTS

a parting letter

Listen! Inside. Can you hear them?
The voices that echo and fall.
Seeping out from the reinforced steel,
and the broken floor in the hall.

Ghosts my friend, they're with you always,
in various guises and forms.
In a house full of whispers,
and pain and regret; walled secrets
where darkness was borne.

They're the creak on the landing,
the running footsteps
that make you jump up from your chair.
But when you arrive, your heart pounding hard,
There's nothing and nobody there.

It's the sound of the laughter,
The splash of the bath,
The deflated bike tyre,
Toy car on the path.
Just open a door and you'll hear his voice,
and her voice, once happy,
'Til you made your own choice.

For in building this house you forgot to build home.
It has no foundations and its heart is of stone.
Its cracks are just plastered and never repaired
The roots spread like cankers in a garden that's dead.

And so here it is now, four walls made of brick;
this asset you fought for and won.
But while you were sniping, you lost sight;
in fighting, your two greatest assets are gone.

Ghosts my friend they'll be with you always.
You will hear them, they'll wrench out your soul.
And my friend, you should fear them,
'til the end of your days;
They're within, like a gaping black hole.

STEPPING OUT
ON DERBY DAY

The moment before I stepped out,
Time arrested;
I saw the future played out before me
like a news reel;
like the life I would not live.

All sound stopped.
There was no chattering crowd,
jostling for a space against the fence.
I did not hear
crashing iron hooves,
or feel the ground's vibration
rise up through my feet,
and into my chest
to compete with my dancing heart,
and the sound of blood pounding
through my swimming head.

The air sizzled with static,
as if earth were anticipating;
bracing for impact.

There was no question
of waiting;
we were meant to meet -
the horse and I -
on this unexpected battlefield.

Not a drawn-out fight;
an almighty explosion of light
and sound, thundering down,
to plough me to the ground,
its rippling body tearing
into mine.

One small step for woman
to change the course of time.

NATASHA

They wonder what her future would have been.
Two grey warriors for justice
carry their evidence in a plastic bag;
fight for what is right;
consumed by pain's white heat,
trying to reconcile love with loss.

Torments them, the unwritten script:
Scientist; Woman; Mother? Wife?
An empty hole;
An unlived life.

Grief meets anger;
unravelling tangles,
uncovering the scandal
of how she asked for help,
which did not come.

Even justice stings;
They scarcely stand, diminished.
Her room a mausoleum of dust, untouched.
In the corner, a pink teddy bear;
a cello with a broken string.

Coroner rules Avon and Wiltshire trust failed in the care of Natasha Abrahart

Neglect by a mental health trust contributed to the suicide of a Bristol University student with severe social anxiety who was found dead on the day she was due to take part in a "terrifying" oral test, a coroner has ruled.

After the inquest, Abrahart's parents also blamed the university, claiming it failed to put in place measures to help their daughter, even though staff knew for six months that she was struggling.

ELEVENTH HOUR

At the eleventh hour, everything
stopped.
Streets fell silent,
shops fell silent,
and silence sat among the men
like a sentinel at a sepulchre.

No whispered voices could be enough to cry
halt to the outpouring of remembrance;
to cry halt to the keen numbness,
as the distance of time dissolves

into deafening chaos, distorted
heat-warped haze with seamless
streams of fiery trails,
endlessly raining down,
as the black sky cracked,
choking, spewing, belching
acrid thunder,
and split the world,
and ripped the whole asunder.

All quiet now.
Few last men standing to tell the tale;

and if they do, it's all the gripping glory
and drunken frolics of camaraderie,
rather than spilling their guts
and fear, to anyone who'll hear.

And if he had not told me, what then?
Only third hand inference from my pen.
A woman to relate that story of countless men.
A generation lied to and lost;
A generation left to count the cost.

I remember this man still.
One lung; the other lost to gas,
struggling to breathe in home fire's burning;
sitting in his chair,
a warm blanket and windows wide to give him air.
He never talked about it much;
never to his child or wife;
thankful that he had a life.

And even then, just six years old, I saw his mind.
And, decades on, because I knew him,
we both are the last of a kind.

APPLE SPLINTER

For Jacob, at 18

When you shot across the bed,
and didn't cry,
wide-eyed,
you looked surprised.
A split-second silence signalled shock
for both parties.
You're here at last.
A lifetime of a second... then
the siren wail began,
blaring out the indignant ignominy of

sudden separation.

You're blue; a boy, a familiar stranger.
I recognised you the moment you arrived.
Would you like to hold him?
Clean him up first.
You're not fragile; you have a barrel chest.
But how do I hold you? I'm afraid
I might break you.

Like handling rare and precious porcelain,
I take you, finally, awkwardly, your

head the wrong side
In my arms.
I gingerly turn you to the right side-
My First Decision.
I don't own you. You eye me with a
knowing nod and wink.
A century old already, you are your own person;
a miniature adult nose; a doll; a perfect form.

I don't own you.
Your face is full of fear the night before.
My gentle euphemisms and encouragements
all undone in one unanticipated question.
You think it's just one day, that place you
go to.
I had to peel you off this morning;
Unripe fruit,
A wrench, drenched with weary tears
tears at me even now.

A stranger has entered the house.

I recognise you - twice my size; unfamiliar shape.

You are fragile.
You still might break.

THE HUNTED DOWN

*"Hunting is not a sport. In a sport, both sides
should know they are in the game."
Paul Roderiguez*

When we run free,
wind nudges at our backs;
our energy a quickening beat,
pulsing with living heat;
darting between shadows;
soft on swift and soundless feet;
bright halo of sun dapples us
with eternal light.

But soon outrun;
left staring down the barrel of a gun;
silent screams dissipate
and run like blood down study walls
that sweat with the stench of dirty money;
coats sported by powdered princesses;
heads hanging high for trophies;
our souls gagged and bound

for the ever-rising mound
of empty, voiceless dead
piled up,
discarded like rubbish,
dismissed
and left for dust.

FOREST

Trees lie fallen, lit by warm winter sun;
a reminder of where wind, in careless fun,
threw them to the floor with abandoned glee.
And over all the silent scene
a silver shadow hangs;
the blanched sun's diluted beams twist
between the boughs left standing,
and bend, fragmented,
to dance lightly over the defeated.

Time was, when only wind made
paths through woods
and disturbed the leaves with gentle breaths.
Now fresh seasons blow relentless gales at times,
and something else is stirring.

The creatures have all left the woods deserted,
and time passes in a heartbeat;
the bleached sun exposing bones from long ago,
that lie dry and impotent,
as it rises white over this embittered isle.

INVASION

I am, at present, invisible.
The naked eye cannot detect
my presence, as I nest, swaddled,
bathed in blood, waiting to grow.

I did not ask to be here,
but I saw a vacancy and
stealthily slipped inside,
insidiously infiltrating, to lie,
dormant.

I wait to grow, gaining strength
from your weakness.
A parasite, I feed on you
like a kite devours its prey.
I grow nourished and
I multiply.

My army marches forth:
all my siblings are perfect
copies of myself,
suckling on the power
of success
from your increasing

failure.

Our infantry makes the final charge
and all of your defences collapse,
bowing to the will of nature's
malevolent, forceful strength
in numbers.
You surrender to attack;
cave-in, until,
Finally,
You
Stop.

WESTMINSTER BRIDGE 2020

Upon Wordsworth's return

Returning to the scene today at dawn,
I wonder that this view deserved a sonnet.
For suddenly I stand, watching
an unfamiliar horizon;
the sun's ruby-tainted orb struggling into sight,
wrapped as in a bloody shroud.
No majesty in these clouds which
herald her appearance
like fallen angels clothed in stained white.

The silent city sleeps still:
but demons stalk the dreams of children
desperate to claw back hours and minutes lost
to time's indomitable stride.

Earth has oft seen long wars hard won;
but facing an invisible enemy,
this city's mighty heart arrests,
and love lies bleeding in the dust;
a far cry from humanity;

when we can only live to hope
of walking hand in hand
where pure skies may yet reign.

FLESH AND GLASS

During lockdown

I imagine your real-life flesh,
pixelated; shattered;

into particles
smaller than dust;

filtered through airwaves,

and re-formed
to meet me, divided

by glass.

My fingertips touch
your hard, flat form;

tracing the valleys
and peaks
of your mapped-out features.

I could get lost in your landscape,
attempting to navigate

this severed connection.

What keeps us going
is knowing
that time will come
when the distance between us dissolves into flesh,
and hands, not voices, overlap;
and eyes, not screens, light up

to guide us back home.

TWO HAIKU

for the seasons

HIDE

Winter's icy hand
Reaches out and drags me down.
Ice distorts my view.

HOPE

Awaiting summer.
The season without which we
Would curl up and die.

TANKA

FAITH

Each tiny droplet
Washes like a birthday song
Over hands that heal
To bless us with a cleansing
To bring us hope as we sing.

CHURCH DOORS

On Thursday,
we drove out to the church
where you married;
the idea to capture
a similar pose
to one fifty years gone.

And I can see you now;
standing in the frame
of the narrow stone arch;
both turned towards the lens,
eyes squinting in the sun,

young,
half-smile, face plumped;
children really;
younger than my own son,
'I do,' done.

After all the singing
and hymns;
they echo still in the dry stone,
where crisp stripes of light
dapple the grass in parts,

which ripple in waves
taken by the whim of wind,
signalling the cusp of season's change.

The archway was always crumbled -
just you didn't notice then;
your stiff-whipped veil
shades you;
his Nehru collar up-turned;

and you tread blithely;
best feet forward;
pick your way between stones
of those who stood, and stood
where you are now,
and then

into a decimal decade
of candles and cuts
rubbish piled up;

Lean times ahead.
But this day,
fifty years gone,
not yet.

Not yet struggled with a daughter,
Abstruse;
ink-haired;
not yet met.

Not had to slow down to mend,
have a heart repaired;

reach sell-by-date,
had the ground around you now
gain more than you have
in a lifetime.

Church door remains
unlocked,
if you want to push it.

Inside,
past the photograph,
blast of sound-proofed
cold
reeks of the old.

Strange that we frame our faith
in pleated stone,
and coloured glass in high windows,
acting out rituals
of nuptials, arrivals,
and exits;

while, outside,
time turns on a photograph
taken today,
And fifty years gone.

SWIMMING

There are those days
when everything falls into place;
where time suspends
in shimmering droplets
falling on a face;
endless cascades,
rippled by calm breeze
and warmed by sun's soft breath.

Maybe a return to water;
A quiet re-birth;
A resurrection of a truth
rising from dry earth
to quell the frantic, never-ending chase;
sure strokes quickening,
propelled by grace
and kicking back to life
in free-form shapes.

WAITED, I DID

Waited, I did
for you to arrive;
for the longest time;

When finally, you were there.
No knock, or bell,
No flurry of noise,
Or trumpet of sound.

More like a silencing;
like mist over dawn;
or the way horizons
quietly suck the sunset down
and away,
like the end of a play.

I realised,
my whole life
I waited.

And how it can lead up to now,
this moment,
is no surprise,
as I watch myself rise,
and peacefully glide;

melt away, like snow.

I see them fret around me,
angry over things I'll never see;
desperate for something to keep, and not forget.
I want to tell them that just an act of kindness,
or a memory,
is all they need,
to nullify regret.

Time, at once moves on,
and stands still;
meaning everything is true,
but nothing real.

It has been decades since
the day I waited,
and centuries since
I first saw a shadow;

And even then I knew
the shadow that I waited for
... was you.

WAITING WATER

a sea shanty

I go down to the waiting water;
I go down to the waiting sea;
I'm the child of a sailor's daughter;
shipwrecked shores - they made me.

And I go down to the water;
I go down to the pale blue sea;
I go down to the water;
I go down to the sea.

Sunset rises over pale moon water;
sunset rises over pale beliefs.
Pale blue eyes over misty water;
pale blue eyes will save me

And I go down to the water;
I go down to the pale blue sea;
I go down to the water;
I go down to the sea.

Take you down to the stormy water,
love to carry you along with me.
Sun-bleached laughter through windy weather
blowing out to rescue me.

And I go down to the water;
I go down to the pale blue sea;
I go down to the water;
I go down to the sea.

Drown your lives in the darkening water;
save your life along with me.
Blow your tears to the misty water;
save your life, sing along with me.

And I go down to the water;
I go down to the pale blue sea;
I go down to the water;
I go down to the sea.

And I go down to the waiting water
I go down to the waiting sea
I'm the child of a sailor's daughter,
shipwrecked shores, well, they made me.

IN MY SHOES

I have walked in many kinds of shoes:

When I was small
they were a perfect fit;
sturdy quality,
parading in dim-lit shops
smelling of dust and leather;
made-to-measure, and fashioned
with love.

And as I grew,
I tried my mother's shoes for size;
towered inches higher;
paper-stuffed the toes;
clip-clopping up the hall
like a new-born foal.

And there were other shoes to come -
ballet pumps,
that took me pirouetting
over quavers; crotchets, with a minim rest;
until I took to dancing to a different tune.

I squeezed my feet
into ankle boots
and kitten heels with pointed toes;

tottered unsteadily,
wiggled like Monroe;
danced 'til 3am in six-inch heels,
and then limped home,
walking wounded;
barefoot; blistered; bleeding,
dodging broken glass and needles;

those shoes you wear returning home
by sunrise,
passing joggers on the way,
gratefully discard them by the bed,
as you crawl in shamefully,
with aching feet and head
as others start their working day.

I change shoes quite often.
Some I keep, like old friends;
some outgrow their use;
some look beautiful,
although they pinch me
and abuse;
some I gave away,
along the way.

The shoes I favour now for comfort
do not mistake for dull;
they shine so brightly!
I walk in them for miles
as I trip lightly
on the roads and paths I make,
I leave behind a trail

of stars and rainbows
in my wake.

I read once about a boot re-patriated;
leg still inside!
back from foreign soil,
to re-unite with owner, long dead.

Such is the power of shoes
to bring us back home.

I will end my days un-shod,
barefoot
when finally I end the merry dance
relieving weary soul,

hoping that my child
will always wear the shoes that fit.

TIM SAUNDERS PUBLICATIONS

publishers of poetry and short stories

"Everybody has a book in them,"

according to journalist
Christopher Hitchens (1949 to 2011)

Do you have a book you would like to publish?

Email. tsaunderspubs@gmail.com
For more information visit:
tsaunderspubs.weebly.com

*We are always on the look out for
poetry and short stories.*

Printed in Great Britain
by Amazon

16546509R00062